Truth or Lie

Truth or Lie

by D.C. Cole

Graphic Design
Art Director-Sally Jaynes

Senior Publisher
Steven Lawrence Hill Sr.

Awarded Publishing House
ASA Publishing Company

A Publisher Trademark Cover page

ASA Publishing Company
Awarded Best Publisher for Quality Books
105 E. Front Street, Suite 205, Monroe, Michigan 48161
United States of America
www.asapublishingcompany.com

All Rights Reserved. No part of this publication may be reproduced, stored in a retrieval system or transmitted in any form or by any means electronic, mechanical, photocopying, recording or otherwise, without the prior written permission of the publisher. Author/writer rights to "Freedom of Speech" protected by and with the "1st Amendment" of the Constitution of the United States of America. This is a work of non-fiction and an academic learning tool for education.

Any resemblance to actual events, locales, person living or deceased is entirely coincidental. Names, places, and characters are within the work of non-fiction and its entirety is from the imagination of its author.

Any and all vending sales and distribution not permitted without full book cover and this title page.

Copyrights©2011, D.C. Cole, All Rights Reserved
Book: Truth or Lie
Date Published: 9.2011
Edition: 1 *Trade Paperback*
Book ASAPCID: 2380571
ISBN: 978-1-886528-04-8
Library of Congress Cataloging-in-Publication Data

This book was published in the United States of America.
State of Michigan

A Publisher Trademark Title page

This book is dedicated to my son, Jaxon Cole. He has been the biggest inspiration to me and my writing of children books.

Truth or Lie

by D.C. Cole

Do you know what a **Lie** is?

Do you know what the **Truth** is?

Let's find out.

My hair is Purple?

Is that a lie or the truth?

I am wearing a hat.

Is that a lie or the truth?

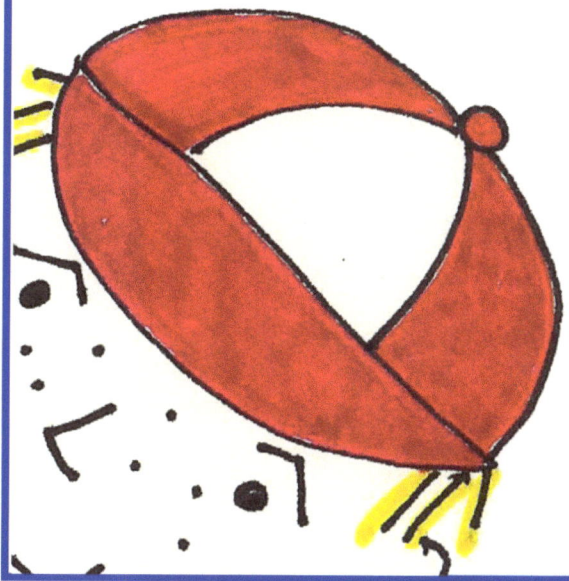

I've seen flying monkeys on my home today.

Is that a lie or the truth?

My favorite food is Brussels Sprouts.

Is that a lie or the truth?

I am a girl.

Is that a lie or the truth?

I always do what my mommy tells me to.

Is that a lie or the truth?

I wear my socks on my feet.

Is that a lie or the truth?

Doing something wrong, and saying someone else did it.

Is that a lie or the truth?

www.ingramcontent.com/pod-product-compliance
Lightning Source LLC
Chambersburg PA
CBHW042128040426
42450CB00002B/118